**More Praise for**

"Tenenbaum's poems are lyrical, tightly woven, at times whimsical. They are powerful poems of a mother's passing, of a brother's face, of a dad's collapse. The natural world of vines, trees, flowers, pawed creatures is strongly present, as is domestic life, and the poet's life as a banjo player and teacher. In this work images are stacked, stitched, and intertwined, making each poem a mesmerizing read, a piece of music."

—Priscilla Long, author of *Holy Magic* and *Crossing Over: Poems*

"With a deep, underlying music, the poems in *The Arborists* reflect the world's detail. Tenenbaum calls hornets 'little cartographers,' writes a biography in banjo, and remembers 'how we used to lose our nozzles.' This is a world to be richly lost in—where a friend says, 'Can I quit my job yesterday?' and the cat is a 'weather report.' *The Arborists* asks what to do with the artifacts of a life, and answers: Craft them into poems."

—Kelli Russell Agodon, author of *Dialogues with Rising Tides*

# THE ARBORISTS

# THE ARBORISTS

Molly Tenenbaum

MoonPath Press

Copyright © 2023 Molly Tenenbaum
All rights reserved.

No part of this publication may be reproduced, distributed, or transmitted in any form or by any means whatsoever without written permission from the publisher, except in the case of brief excerpts for critical reviews and articles. All inquiries should be addressed to MoonPath Press.

Poetry
ISBN 978-1-936657-75-9

Cover art: untitled by Frances Thompson

Author photo by Tom Collicott

Book design by Tonya Namura, using Collaborate (display) and Adobe Caslon Pro (text).

MoonPath Press, an imprint of Concrete Wolf Poetry Series, is dedicated to publishing the finest poets living in the U.S. Pacific Northwest.

MoonPath Press
PO Box 445
Tillamook, OR 97141

MoonPathPress@gmail.com

http://MoonPathPress.com

*for David, Dan, and Kim*

## TABLE OF CONTENTS

Bald-Faced Hornets Eating the Porch — 5
April 4–June 18 — 6
The Arborists — 8
There Was No One Moment — 10
The Stone World — 12
Clematis H.F. Young — 13
After She Died, I Saw the Skull in Everyone — 14
Nine-Year-Old Girl Meets Picasso's Weeping Woman with a Handkerchief — 15
Banjo, Banjo on the Wall — 17
My Father Would Have Loved the Internet — 19
We Used to Lose Our Nozzles All the Time — 21
My brother's face — 23
Do We Gripe? — 26
The Horses' Heads — 29
The White Wing — 31

To an Aunt in Another City — 35
Works on Paper, 1933-2014 — 36
Heard from Inside the Ashes Box — 38
Before Storing Her Paintings under My Bed — 39
Well, she died with them under her own bed, — 40
Pass the Salt — 41
I'm Tired of Life and Death — 43

| | |
|---|---|
| But a Cat Is Always in the Room | 44 |
| Delaying the Book | 46 |
| The Bigger Picture, with Warnings | 49 |
| I Need a Hummingbird | 53 |
| Couple Eating Oranges after Dinner | 54 |
| I Can't Put Enough Household Objects in This Poem to Equal Your Wonderfulness | 56 |

| | |
|---|---|
| Starting Ahead of Time | 61 |
| Equation | 62 |
| The person in the box is the one | 64 |
| O Pie of Grace | 65 |
| Everywhere in the House | 67 |
| How We Say Good Night After a Long Day of Work | 69 |
| Lying Awake Next to a Noisy Sleeper | 71 |
| What I Have Instead | 73 |
| Woman Going Gray | 75 |
| How Long Have You Been Teaching Banjo? | 77 |
| Clematis Miss Bateman | 80 |
| What Have You Not Done Yet? | 81 |
| What to do with a box of folders, | 83 |
| In My Dream It's Always a Wooden House | 95 |
| There Will Be Beauty | 87 |
| They Find Me | 89 |

Notes 91
Acknowledgments 95
About the Author 97

# THE ARBORISTS

## BALD-FACED HORNETS EATING THE PORCH

In old gray wood
    so soft a fingernail
can scribble it, they've bitten
    new tan trails.
Little cartographers,
    chiseling maps
by subtracting the actual
    land of the map.
From my house, they scrape
    their house
and hang it from my house,
    their house whose door
looks like the hole
    a blunt pencil goes in.
In my house, the scraping's
    of teeth with floss,
of carrots with a rough brush,
    of the brain,
for the hornets
    chewing in there,
while these other
    pencil-faced oblivions
of me go sharp and busy
    all day about
their laminations.

## APRIL 4–JUNE 18

Season of when at sixty miles an hour
we flumed by the wall
high enough *Oh no no no*
for her to hide her face with her hand

Of her relief at the doctor's ruling No chemo
no cutting too late
Of her saying *I'm done* and frequently
*This is shit for the birds*

Of red rhododendron lapping in wavelets at the window
Of clematis blue tinsel sparking like shocks

Of her listing to the right and me singing
*Are you listing are you listing*
to the tune of Frère Jaques
*I'm not listing* she said but she was

Of the hospice booklet's question for reflection
What have you not done yet
*I have not yet loved you enough*

Of a glass of wine a spoonful of wine the tiniest
slipper of wine

From the bowl of the yard brimming silver with shotweed
one sharp thistle spangling up

Of nothing beginning or ending
the rhody's gummy brown flowers
rain-pasted flat on its own clacking leaves

Of expensive thick steak in the freezer
she'd planned ahead for her final treat

still burning there beyond
the last food she could eat

## THE ARBORISTS

The arborists catch a thin line
as it comes down, swing it up, a line
with red weight on the end,
swing again, and this time
over a branch, which branch, the one
they'd arched heel to head backwards
to point to, squinting and shading.
Tie heavy blue rope
to the line, heave and heave,
and up in the branches
the rope disappears.

Cinch their leg-loops, buckle
their helmets, check their tension—
clicking ascenders, they raise themselves,
the rope raises them, they're raising the rope,
they are rising.

Now they're a glimpse and shift
in drifting branches, brief white
plastic pate, denim flash, chainsaws
afloat, the engine-sound dense
in wood, or spacious and swaying,
shimmer of feather-blue rope,
and up where stormed branches
hung fibrous, one gust away
from the neighbor's roof,
new rounds flat as stepstones
nimble the trunk, the saws
shaping and rolling like emery.

When had by loop swung down, had been up,
swaying, but down now, and coil by coil
vanishing rope in a red nylon bag, the bag

hauled between them to the truck.
No more in the branches, sky-blank
helmet, cone-brown boot.
They're sweeping with brooms
on the walk, tossing twigs in the back.
Throwing a long arc, brooms landing on top.

The fired-up motor's shaking the one in the cab,
and one's on the walk, nodding, handing a slip,
*Thank you, thanks* for the check, their exhaust
of unburned gas, the sound dense and spacious,
peaceful and small, turning, now turned,
entered into the spooling arterial.
Where now, who swayed in the tree, denim
and darted? Where now, been and gone.

## THERE WAS NO ONE MOMENT

There was no one moment before which
lived, after which, died.
A day and long night
of foam in the throat, of hands in the air
as if testing the fineness of sheets,
of two words, *I want* ____, the foam like yeast
bubbling into the blank, the hands
already ghosts come to say one last thing,
if they could just think of it, as if hands
in their transparent garments could speak.
A night of turns, my brother and I,
one to dream, one to time the drops.
My turn awake, I rocked and read, page
turning page, even now, wanted to know
was the jewel buried
with the body, had someone
taken the money, would the girl get away
or be stuck in this small town forever,
though maybe there's no either/or—if
there was a moment, I missed it,
a hiss, looked up
as an out-breath, the force
of it, lifted her eyebrows,
sat her straight up, expelled
a surprised *Oh*, dropped her back,
was it then—but when? during
the lift, the *Oh*, the fall?—
and it wasn't a *then*,
it was a pane of water in a glass—
the cat leapt on the bed,
and my brother before his hour
loomed down the hall, shadow first,
one of us, then the other, touching her face,
if it felt alive, one then the other

touching her neck, if a pulse moved,
one then the other, ear to her lips,
if a soft song of breath, for hours,
while soft through the window the breathing
of lemony rose-petal June.
Until seven, with two pages left,
our own nurse on shift
hugged us, reminded, remove the rings,
emptied the pills to a gallon bag,
poured in water—then?—and cups of cat litter.
Until my friend, with a handful of grasses
and yellow pink flowers gathered
from yards on the way,
laid the bouquet on her breast,
on the white sheet, so young,
as if her hair were long and spread,
as if a lace gown,
though short and gray, though only a sheet,
while we sat together, and my friend
sang slow words in another language
to tell the spirit not to be confused,
that this was the way, this the scented air
to enter and become.

## THE STONE WORLD

The lawns still the lawns
the fallen leaves
the coils from the dogs

The trees still the trees
and the air itself
rushing and cool

I could go on
listing all that's the same
today's walk

as before but
however it looks
it's gone mineral

Wrens and their chinking
now stone and a stone breeze
lifting the branch and the crows

Squirrels and their tails gone granite
gone quartz the bark dust
that drifts in the sun

though we were watching
all night
though we never changed

yesterday's clothes
still clean not even
a speck

# CLEMATIS H.F. YOUNG

This dimple flower shorting out violet, this flower scrambling radio, this fizz on blue fire kitchen match, this flower woke up alive started screaming.

This pool this deep, how deep, this deep, this flower going all iris at the edges, this flower rippling out to the spires of trumpets, this stoneflower falling and falling.

This flower soft *pat pat*, this yellow plush, this wind-up gizmo, this sharp amethyst, anxious, who are we kidding is the anxious one here, this flower drank five cups of black tea, this flower knife of a flower, this flower cut flat to dirt will bloom.

This flower doesn't know anything, this blue maze, killer cocktail, blue jay shrieking this coldhearted planet, this flower all innocent skyface, if it were an ashtray, kitsch, this tickle of granny facepowder, dish of hard candy, come closer, give us a kiss, now just try to find your way home.

## AFTER SHE DIED, I SAW THE SKULL IN EVERYONE

Who knew skulls came in such colors—
I counted those moving toward me,
paint chips for subtle interiors,
Meteor, Blue Milk, The Coo of the Dove.

Each moving toward me, Rosy Finch,
a flash of Golden Trout.
One of powdery Overcooked Yolk,
and Brown Scorch, like hot iron on a sheet.

And still coming, but which
is the last I shall see, the crowds
continuously approaching?

In the mirror, there's mine,
that underground cave
in Smoke Horses
I nod with my crystals and yellows,

*Hello*, with my cavern careening stone tools
across the floor's tilt while you speak,
our thoughts, the scrape,
our talk, a paint of burnt pine.

## NINE-YEAR-OLD GIRL MEETS PICASSO'S WEEPING WOMAN WITH A HANDKERCHIEF

    Los Angeles County Museum of Art, circa 1966

You were the first I saw with pupils knots of hard black thread
first with two eyes frontward but inward in opposite paisleys
first eyelashes like two nail tufts and one bar of dynamite

first I saw facing me turning aside
your profile nose plus two squirmy nostrils
yours the first black arrow as the middle of a face

yours the first teardrops on wires
your tears that would swing and clack together
your headwear scored like a long loaf of bread
here's where to break into slices

you the first time I didn't know my own question
something like How do eyes swim to the side
is my question and Will I
also have knots in my eyes
yours the first real pain I saw
so my question is How
can a line say a feeling    my question
is How did the painter remember to not paint
the cheek where it vanishes under the eye

purple blotch in your chin
can that be a question
or maybe he painted the whole cheek first
and the top-layer eye on it later

what shape tomato soup what color tuna sandwich
flecks of lavender there
my mother and I in wire chairs by a window

by water that smells like mastodons
the buildings afloat on the green squares of fountain
my question is How to stop thinking the gills
of your neck your fingers thick as paint tubes
and on your hand under the handkerchief
your fingers never had to be painted at all

you the first time my mother couldn't see inside me
first time I became nothing she knew
shadow behind you with gashes of white

my mother's green-and-black dress and gold belt
lapped metal I used to bend so the scales hackled up
my question is Underneath this one
do I have another real face

since then they've re-done the museum
the tar wouldn't stop seeping up in the fountain
it's all walkways now and more changes planned
removing the room where I saw you
the new design draws from the fluid forms of the tar
they say and they say from the air
the new buildings will look like an inkblot
my question is To whom does that view matter

you taut cloth with paint on top
you square like a window casting a patch on the floor
one might stand where it hurts
my question is giving up
you my first triangle neck my first yellow slope shoulders
one roll of your hair a red fan the blades outlined in black

## BANJO, BANJO ON THE WALL

How do you even begin banjo?
Don't dare play my banjo. I'm leaning it here
while I'm out ploughing banjo.
Teenage banjo in her room, a little bird told me a banjo.
Why do you fly so high, wings so blue banjo?
I come with cramped hands and a cheap plastic banjo.

Oh my dear porch rail, splintering banjo.
Oh, put a sock in your daydreaming banjo.
Hello, my name is Slaughter banjo.
Is that a cakepan or a human skull banjo?
Can I play your sugarpast banjo?

Dunno, I just play banjo.
Knock knock. Banjo.
Flesh hoop, calfskin.
What inlay's engraved
on the hidden heel of your banjo?

I have seen a cat's ass banjo, Pleiades banjo,
banjo overgrown with vines.
Never no more lighthouse banjo, never
no more poppy, paintbrush,
coastal wildflower banjo.

This banjo dents my breasts.
This banjo tore my shorts.
Try a padded, stonewashed banjo.

This banjo a baker, this banjo cold iron,
this banjo crisping out creed.
Can a banjo be vegetarian?
What is the sound of a lentil banjo?
Loosen the head and rattle your banjo,

full-moon banjo, fry up
your all-night, bacon-fat banjo.

Tighten the brackets and bright up your banjo,
high-bridge banjo. Even on an island,
one will make a banjo. Banjo of dawn,
banjo of dew. Don't be nostalgic,
You Tube, Soundcloud, tattoo banjo,
walnut, cherry, while yet there be trees—

what will grow if you plant your banjo? Do you
play ekonting banjo? If Heaney had a banjo.
This blackberry banjo, soft in the rain.
This California banjo, burning banjo,
smoky terroir of the banjo,

this living banjo clock counting down
(*How do you know when to end?* outsiders ask
the huddled banjos), counting up
to thirty-two or three parts or
one extra beat, hard stop, though the mineral
tang of the short string dies on.

## MY FATHER WOULD HAVE LOVED THE INTERNET

He'd have looked up ads for Thoreau's pencils,
blue box, green box, drawing pencils, *best quality*,
carpenters' pencils, round or oval.
Curious at *ptarmigan*, he'd link to more *pt*:
We want to protect our *pterions*, the H on the skull
where sutures meet. What's tangential,
he'd ask. *Pterna*, the bone of the heel,
so near to *ptero*, winged. And when the wings
of our eyes fall out, *ptilosis*. The world
has come to this: *ptochogony*, creation
of a class of poor people. *Ptui*.
He who browsed paper, who did love
to hear a page turn, who loved pages
for the size of them to hide his face.
Whose dictionary to settle an argument
was in the other room. Who loved a chance
to go to the other room. You can sleep
with a page on your face. The print, the taste.
But he'd have loved the internet
for its list of palindromes, its anagram server,
He of the unmeant trombone. He of the tenderest,
up in the night with the cat videos.
He could be in a series of too-small boxes.
He could be in a map of Descanso Gardens,
by the sagebrush at the corner turn.
He could be on You Tube, alive
in the 1973 faculty talent show.
To turn is to swipe.
To keep is to bookmark.
He could be in the next room, sleeping,
his lips in and out, a video playing
of lips in and out. In the internet,
he's clicking to the Hubble Deep Field,

*click*, Deep Field South, *click*, and confirm
the universe is uniform on a large scale,
my small-scale papa with his miniature
black-framed lenses. Passwordless.
A burnt memento? No.
*Oh*, he says, *Turn a bone moment.*
*Oh*, he says, *Bemoan men, nut ort.*
Scraps from a meal,
fodder remaindered by cattle,
fragment of wisdom or wit.
Oh my Ort folder, where I drag and save my bits.

## WE USED TO LOSE OUR NOZZLES ALL THE TIME

We used to lose our nozzles
all the time, front yard, back yard,
one hose end so like another,
when the neighbor's lettuce
sizzled on our summer dime,
when our dig to plant the frayed
pet fish caved in. *Come,*
*you stains and sputters,*
Mom was calling, so we dropped them,
*whomp*, in their little dirt footprints,
dinner a spray of crumbs and melted butter.
We dipped, and dipped so well.
Just then, someone changed
the subject, someone went
to college, some one of us
seemed older so we stood
aside and never invented the rest.
Our stories had wanted
to invent themselves, but all
we gave them for matter
was minutes and pulses of heat.
We wanted to give them
a good night's sleep, but all night,
swayed among themes.
When we'd tried to soak deeply,
we sluiced the dirt to the driveway
to dry like waves
we'd sweep and wreck.
There'd been a dial for Fan, Shower, Jet.
Center dug up roots.
Gentle was never enough.
Took so long, we stopped

before full slake, and later,
so many shrubs it could be under.

## MY BROTHER'S FACE

looks like a face in pain, but this is his resting face.
How can he bear it, here at Gate A2?

He looks like a man suffering in a painting, bearded man
with blade or nail, deathbed man, mouth

moaning from hell's crowded pool.
His grim jaw could crack. He's just reading his book.

We've been to Berkeley, friends who love us,
we love them, we're going home, love home,

keep saying *Kitties soon*. Yet his face a dire block
as if having just heard a doctor's report.

Face of I can't bear it, face of I will break,
face of This is bearing it, actual news days later

when five die in the crash on the bridge,
students at my school, young from their countries,

had only yesterday said goodbye to their parents. How can
their parents bear it? And forty more injured.

*Counselors and faith-based professionals will be on hand,*
said the campus email. *It is with heavy heart*

*I bring this tragic news*, said our college president,
and we centered ourselves in his upstanding suit,

his declarative sentence. My school's architecture is Brutalist—
by which we mean softened in fall's orange-speckled green ivy,

and maples whistling their million pointy leaf-tips
on all the stairs and walks as we begin.

My brother alone in his airport chair,
the Brutalist bones of his face, large and square,

gray beard to soften his cheeks. Little brother
who would eat only carrot sticks, skinny boy brother,

best teller of jokes. His resting face a house of cloud
from which expressions emerge and pass

like cloud shadows on mountains.
Like how, in the night, we know it's raining:

the cat comes in wet. Wet are the faces
of some who received calls and some who did not.

What is the time and place?
It is before boarding.

We're listening for our rows.
We're anxious for room in the overhead

for our tender instruments, handcarved wood.
We tag behind MVP Gold, say, *We're with him*.

We want to be first. What is the time and place?
In the meeting at school:

*Our college community extends our support.*
I'd had to laugh at one bit on the news—

last year, the board, re-branding, cut *Community*
from our name, but in this disaster, the reporter returned it.

And now, our president's voice claims it too.
Last winter, though, I refrained from Reply-All

when he promoted it, proclaiming Seahawks Week.
Wear the blue shirts! Let blue flags fly from all office doors!

We're a college, not a commercial.
What is a faith-based professional?

My brother and I are professionals. We're alive.
What is the place and time?

His eyes dark as black shoes.
If you saw someone with that face, you'd ask, *Can I help?*

*What?* he'd say. *I'm just reading my book.*
Going home to where in two days the Duckmobile

will slam the divider and crush the bus.
Where in two days the cat's xray

will show a possible growth, but the radiologist will say,
*No, it's just thickness and shadow.* Said a pedestrian

on the bridge, *It looked like war, the bodies everywhere.*
They took them to the nearest wide place,

Woodland Park Zoo, and sorted them there
for hospital, for home. To the cat,

my brother's face, so high up, is a ghost,
and one human face like another, but she knows

his key in the door, that he's home with his voice,
his breath, his lap, his tears of love raining down.

## DO WE GRIPE?

    Letter to Martha, October

Let's keep the subject line, remnant of didn't-win bitching.
The pizza was amazing, pear and gruyère,

a tongue of salty prosciutto. Every night, at least three
readings, releases, parties, with, if I went, quick

turnsaround after work and only grabbed snacks for dinner.
So I stay home, but miss who might have known me.

Can we be still? In the kitchen, I listened
to a prompt for winter evening: thirty minutes,

watch the sunset. My window aims east and steams up.
So I chop and listen to radio linguists, call-ins questioning

family usage: "What's it mean, my granny's phrase
at someone's sneeze: *Scat cat, your tail's in the fire?*"

The salad of lemon-dressed romaine.
Cancer of the pancreas. All I know is people live longer now

than when my dad, with no diagnosis till collapse,
lived one more week. Before that, three years

of complaint, doctors missing the meaning.
A friend's sister has lived so far some seven years,

and another's mother hasn't died yet after five,
which her daughter, my friend, measured by her own

mastectomy, chemo, recurrence.
Now gone beyond measure. A side effect

is depression, but my dad was depressed before.
Selenium and lycopene sound like a little song.

Your friend, the judge and pilot—her life,
what will it have been? Lycopene, that's apricots and plums.

And beets, but the word sounds like wolves.
Selenium's a mineral, what once they left out of cat food

until the cats started dying. *Scat cat*, you never
know what's essential. A game I play

is how short a time to live before I quit cleaning the house.
A year as I blur under dust?

A six-month prognosis the cut-off
beyond which dishes crust? A week? A day?

Says David, *Maybe you'd be cleaning right to the end.
Maybe that's what you'd like to be doing.*

To rest with the smoothness and shining.
I used to believe—not believe, really, but dream—

not dream, really, but see—a sunny place like a patio,
geraniums in flowerpots, nasturtiums trailing,

a mint-bed nearby in damp shade,
and there I'd be, finally, somehow,

with enough money and a long afternoon.
Can I quit my job yesterday?

Really, I'm happy looking at trees.
I'll never become a complete person.

When I'm dead, that will have been my life.
Was it a thing? Did it start at a point, did it complete?

My own arm hits me in the middle of sleep.
I'll ask to be sung to and read to.

I'll want to drift and hear voices.
At summer camp, summer of the moon landing,

in the cabin with the other girls, the moon for the first time
with a footprint on it, the rattlesnake under the floorboards,

to be aware at at the moment of falling,
to know what happens in my eyes, my breath,

I'd lie on my back with my arm in the air, and wait
for its drop to tell me, *Now*—

the plop from state to state. Breakfast bell,
and we're down to the lodge by the orchard,

each assigned a table and place. No one could start
until the couple who'd founded the camp had entered:

Grover, straight and silvered, Erma, curly, with her cane.
They'd stand at the head of Table One until we stood too—

their sitting down, permission for us to lower before
our family-style bowls, beginning the rhythm, lifting
    our spoons.

## THE HORSES' HEADS

Because I could not stop,
I stepped onto my rolling plat,
scored paths for gardens,
dashes for streets. Sketched trees,
but the green so enmeshed,
I erased, for ease of seeing,
every other branch.
Always beneath my beat,
my feet spinning
white as hot water.
Always behind my eyes,
an onion unwrapping,
advancing to dinner. Since
Can't stop's corollary
is Can't go back,
it's too late, this winter, to crush
one more fragrant footprint down
last summer's thyme stairs.
Because I could not stop,
I drank strong tea so my heart
would race when I sat still.
When I sat still, I clamored
fast music. All in a rumble
for round, for ripe, I'd tested the soil,
fed the plot, slurped as many Sweet Millions
as were halfway red, could not stop,
the juice eating sores in the silver skin
of my mouth. The hurrying house,
it wants my life savings
for a new roof,
though the instant I exit,
investors will scrape it, doorstep

to cornice, clean off its dirt
to plop a bigger one
on what had been my lot.

## The White Wing

At my ear, left ear, a moth
    won't brush away.
Floating blur, white wing,
    friend or foe of my face,

    we are going out walking, we're going.

A bit of fluff, a whiff
    of paper, small white sound,
a foot-caught bird. What is it,
    floating here, white blur?

    We are going out walking.
    Tell them, tell them, we're going.

White hair of my head,
    white wing at my eye,
Whatever you tell me
    to do I do.

    We are going out walking,
    Tell them, tell them, we're going.

## TO AN AUNT IN ANOTHER CITY

You weren't choosing a croissant
nor pressing peaches for their give and swell,
and though you'd tried two florists, on your stroll,
you hadn't found a bright enough bouquet,
so not at bakery nor stall, but home,
crossing from bed to 911.
And though it wasn't me you called,
you called, and who came
called the number on the wall.
There was no trick to lure the cat. We grabbed,
and she hid farther back.
We'll take you later up the ridge.
For now, we light the incense sticks we found.
At the bakery, after we'd flown down,
emergency contacts hidden in our phones,
we looked like people eating scones.

## WORKS ON PAPER, 1933-2014

We canceled paper, we shredded paper,
we schlepped bags and bags of paper.
We signed paper, we set aside paper,
we answered and asked paper.
She was not there, but she was on paper.
There was color on paper and a mountain and a tomato.
Everyone was asking about the paper.
*What are you doing with the paper?*
*Can we have some of the paper?*
She would have liked the one about the paper
cowboy wanted for rustling.
Paper made us laugh. We wanted
to scan her phone-pad paper
sketches of collars and hairdos on cards and mail them.
Is there a stamp for this paper?
And the rates, haven't they risen?
We wrote Return to Sender on paper.
We paid a grand, shipping ourselves her truckload of paper.
At home, we tossed our own paper,
summer camp paper, college paper,
Sorry, biographers, leap through the gaps in our paper.
She liked real paper, how ink spread and sank in the paper.
If we digitize it, can we keep all the paper?
To digitize means our fingers
split dry from handling the paper.
We wanted to edit what seemed irrelevant paper,
money paper, worry paper,
but she never knew in scratching the paper,
rent check or sunset, which
the last completing paper.
We should show experts the paper.
Collectors would love the best paper.
Would advise to throw out the damp-damaged paper,

spotted like yellow seeds dropped on the paper.
She never knew what to do with the paper,
under her bed, rolled-up paper,
but kept on painting the paper,
never had space to display the paper,
too pricey to frame all the paper,
there is no frame, or now our whole house
around boxes of it is the frame, come over
to see her ocean paper,
what could we do, so much paper, we pushpinned
one piece to the wall, the sun on a mountain on paper.

## HEARD FROM INSIDE THE ASHES BOX

Dull cardboard of a photo propped,
bottom edge a woody thunk,
top edge a click at the plastic wall of the box.

The flesh of a hand sweeping air,
the swish of a vase removed—
the faucet on and off some rooms away—
and shuffling rearrangements here.

Something glass, with a heavy base.

The ant-feet of dust.
A match-strike and incense suspending its ash.

A boot-clunk on a springing floorboard—
and clay beads rattle their dish.
When a door shuts, a wave
through the casters to the top of this cabinet
claps this box to the wall.

I once studied stars and knew mountains.
I once painted blue and black ink,
the moon tangled in pines.

I once watched the fish in the pond
a whole afternoon
and thought I'd wasted time.

## BEFORE STORING HER PAINTINGS UNDER MY BED

I cleaned under the bed four times.
One, with broom.
Two, with vacuum.
Three, with microfiber glove.
Four, with dampened rag
for sands that three had missed.
Thus overshot by one
the wishes number, though
it was a three-day task
to pack her work
in three protections—
foamcore, paper, bubble wrap—
until her life of art,
all brown kraft and plastic air,
heaped like a recycle pile.

By then more motes
had gathered underbed,
so again I cleaned in four
gradations, coarse to fine,
broom to buffed with water,
total of eight, too even
a number ever to shimmer
in soul or surprise,
and three is too many
layers of wrappings to drop like a robe
to stand bare in full portrait,
radiant in the bracing air,
though her life itself
was the bracer, and the magic
is in my hand,
wet as a cloud and smudged
with tiny dust.

## WELL, SHE DIED WITH THEM UNDER HER OWN BED,

died with a thousand single-stroke circles
in a newsprint stack, died with ten pages
of not-quite ducks, their backs a press
with the fat of the brush, their bellies
bare eggshell paper. Died with two red-wattled
black and white chickens, their foreground,
gray chickenwire hints, a few yellow grasses—
a masterpiece mashed under stacks
of calligraphy grids, story of when she wailed
she never would get it, her teacher
cheerily, *Don't worry, do a hundred tonight,*
*bring me the best one tomorrow.*
Which page was tomorrow's? She died with the great
Western mountains on scrolls in the dark
in cardboard tubes, her foam bed
on a plywood plank above bleeding
magenta beets and fiercely gold-veined chard.
We will all die and pass our beds on, next person
lie dreaming on a flat in a frame
above our packets, starting up midnights
to label *trees* or *animals* in black marker
on the brown paper, returning
to slide between thin cottons and under
thick wools back to sleep.

## PASS THE SALT

I was never going to say *passed* for *died*
I'd be direct with the dirt say *I'm sorry she's dead*

My friend listing on eBay her childhood
Barbie's Dream Kitchen

in the Dream drawer the tiny forks
on the Dream table the breakfast with the half-inch
    coffee service

And listing her girlhood toy horses
the black with the white mane still here

while the mare with her foal palomino
was first to sell

We were pouring real wine into real crystal glasses
rushing the red to the bowl's widest slice

the salad on a green-glazed platter
just brought from her mother's

An attic to empty the clues adding up
until it phrased through me *Did your mom pass*

and I joined the long line
the hats of black netting jiggling as they talk

the men so kind in white shirts
the hands clasped in front or shaking yours

as they passed before family kissing their cheeks
We passed the Montepulciano

I passed on seconds of pie
The no-mother air breath by breath

passing through our bodies
We passed the empty plates to the end

A wineglass broke as it passed to the dishwasher
and later we uncased our instruments passing through

the four-chord to five back to one
passing three tunes to the ceiling

Maid of the House Wild Horses High Dad in the Morning
And driving home I nearly passed my own exit

but swerved last minute into my lane
slept in my own bed and so passed the night

I had passed on buying the white-maned black horse
passed on the chance for Barbie's Dream Kitchen

though still I longed for it a little
so tiny and perfect

but for missing
one cup from the coffee service

## I'M TIRED OF LIFE AND DEATH

I want the product where the manufacturer's label
says all man-made fibers.
The item completely
understandable, shining
forward off the stainless rollers.
Utterly seamless,
emitting a homogenous glow.

If once a larval tube
groped for soil;
or if, emerging, a sticky
green eye like an infection
trembled at the top—
I want the object buffed
to the unified hardness below.

When hot fur
breathed in a burrow, when paws
smelled strongly of paw—
a slurry soaked the matter
to molecular components.
I want it fresh from the extruder.

We were keeping the room empty.
The bowl of light on the sill.

To be pure block,
replication removed,
in the slight scent
of flame retardant.
To be in the solid quiet
of the original box.
Unopened,
in mint condition.

# BUT A CAT IS ALWAYS IN THE ROOM

"There can't even be a cat in the room."
—Mary Ruefle, craft talk, October 2017,
Frye Museum, Seattle.

Disguised as a loaf, a lumped sweater.
A dictionary, dim on the stand in the corner.
The room with a coiled breathing center,
tiny sneeze like salt over the shoulder.

Always entering the room, the weather report
of the cat, bushel of mist, brush of pine.
And always the refrain, *Where have you been?*
A walking cat blurs the bottom edge of every scene.

Audible in the room, a delicate thirst tapping the surface.
In the air layer nearest the floor, stink of little dried meats.
Always a hunch, on the rug by the couch,
what's under there, something far back, something
    deep down—

On the windowsill, alert for movement,
watching opposite apartments, watching the park, river,
alert for movement, chasing it into the corner, patting it,
eating the spider.

Stamped on the dark, a cat's silhouette.
A cat's face over the hole where sleep's breath comes out,
a cat asleep on the neck of sleep, sleep
with cat's weight on its chest, sleep turning over
as the weight lifts.

And stuck in the chair-arm like a mending pin,
white crescent of a claw's discarded sheath.
A cat is always in the room, inhabiting the shapes.
The book and lamp. A paw, having stepped
in the paintwater jar, always smearing the periphery.

## DELAYING THE BOOK

Before I'm in the whorl or pin, stray or fall
    of your first sentence, before
        I dissolve to the second,
before I'm out of choices, on the fire-rope
    of your third, in the rockets
        of your *Once upon*, before I've let
myself even glance at Chapter One's initial cap
    which already I know sways
        its wild serifs beyond their block,
let me hold back. Let me hold just
    the Preface, warm brick, and wait.

Let me lift the Foreword to the light, turn it
    like a wineglass for legs, climb columns
        of Contents for the view, from here,
a calm array of short and long.

Let Introduction orient me
one emboldened heading at a time.

Backtrack to title, what year, what art,
    what city, I'm shaking you
        for grocery lists, for whose
flattened freckles of toast,
    whose oily transparencies, fanning fast
        for the air of you, moted or clear, eyefall
on footnotes—those little islands,
    little asides, the safely small blocks

in tight type. Those first,
the tangents and facts.

I'm shutting you up, I'm hoisting for heft,
    for how rocky or rolling my hours shall be in you,
        for what to bring in the long night of you,
for what I can weigh of the dust, the horse, the thirst in you,
    for what you will ask—
        me to be my most limpid, and I will have to,
yes, lay down self-deception,

but first, prying for gossip in *The author would like to thank*
                              of you,
    names of librarians delving for you, archive, carrel, physical
        crick in the neck of you, is there a dog, and who is it
*without whom this book would not…*

I'm checking the colophon, twice, anything
    to not yet start, not yet, the font, designed 1930,
        to give me more time as today's self
at your blank last page, where, next time
    I'll be in the bell of your final word,
        with no more extras, not even errata,

then back to page one to begin disappearing,
    all night, all day, in the book
        that does and doesn't end, will it hurt,
will they find my nightie flat on the couch in the morning,
    will there be drought,
        will the horse die, and someone
says *No, the book itself is water,*
    *a cool living drink, the book is the gallop forever,*
        but I'm loping ahead to when
I've read you ten times, the end's no surprise,
    I'm looking up, it's foggy out, it's early, late,

                    we've lived our long lives, made our pact,
are taking hands to jump.

There's some pink in the sky, and blue-gray blobs like
                                        old gum,
        a black tree looms out, page one,
                page one, and the only way out's in the wisp
of the turning, whistle of shush,
        matter in its atoms never still, and even the closed book
                a stormwind, a huge creaking branch, loud, loud,
frail window, last page
        seems missing though here in black print's
                the last dot. I'm all dots. I lost
my body but someone in this room
        is suddenly very hungry.

# THE BIGGER PICTURE, WITH WARNINGS

    1.
Into the bigger picture,
I'm putting scenes that insomniacked me,
so if you're subject to tossing, if scenes
of human-hurt animals stick on repeat,
STOP READING HERE,
as I wish I had, but smack on a first page

sea turtles minus the plastron
the poachers cut out
crawled still alive
to the sea, eggs falling
loose on the sand.

I'm putting those turtles in the bigger picture
and the poachers too. In a tiny corner,
those shreds of shirt?
The poachers' gull-pecked death.

    2.
In the bigger picture, the sun
has gassed up and absorbed the earth.

Did it hurt?
Don't worry, solar systems can't feel.

    3.
In a poem so short I'd read it before I could not,
a cow minds its own grassy business when
from over the fence for no reason the poem ever says
SKIP THE NEXT LINE
a neighbor stabs a steel spike in its eye.

I've hauled the man to the compactor, pulled the lever.
Now he's not seen in the stamped lower left,
and the cow grazes steppes among aurochs.

    4.
In a huge painted canvas facing the entry,
a center white stallion reared up
STOP HERE IF YOU NEED TO
a spear in his chest and the blood—

That horse and his screaming lips
and the other horses writhing with spears in their bellies,
and also the men with their black mouths
are going into the bigger picture
of the tar pit before the museum was built,
and I'm a child miniaturized in a brochure
where visitors fleck the floors, browsing art.

    5.
I was reading about all five
of our amazing senses, hit taste,
when here's a live monkey STOP NOW
bolted in place, his open skull
under a hole in the table,
his pulsing brain eaten with spoons.

Shall that go in the picture of *Aren't Humans Funny?*
The picture of *Look What They Eat?*

    6.
I tell you, the universe was there.
I'm putting the universe in the bigger picture,
I'm using its brains for paint.
Don't worry, universes can't feel.

7.
Being smashed hurts the insect
only a small-picture moment—he cracks,
pulps out through his splinters—
now he's the blush in the bigger picture,
and cochineal's such a great red.

8.
Here I've been put in the bigger picture.
Over here, head down on the table.
I'm asleep, someone's reading the beautiful sounds,
and the sounds make a sort of big picture
as when the volume's low on the news,
the news a soft singing of voices.

9.
The universe was there,
The universe saw it all.
The universe can't even see.

10.
They know I'm hoarding my mother's gold ring
in my secret small picture.

They, the stars and laws.
They, the asteroid and dinosaurs.

11.
I'd like a middle picture,
sized between my life and the sun,
in which I only briefly
POSTPONE READING ON
in the poem whose second line
says *crucified a cat to a tree*

since the cat and cruel boys have been set
in the poem's bigger picture,
the poem in the book,
and the book soon
returned to the library.

## I NEED A HUMMINGBIRD

A whirring bright and a quick sharp right here,
right here, a fist of hunger, here
gold and neon, need something small
eighty times a second, a blur
that flies backwards, a shimmer at once
green and vermilion. Need
what may be desperation, can't
tell by looking, may be
color and sugar. I need something
from the beginning, continuously
starving to death. Please, a glow, here,
and here, a nest of fine spider hair.
Need a dip, a bead, repeated
prickings, a series of clicks
by which like can find like. Need something,
something, a thing that moves. A burr
in the air, a flame, a little light, something
going going breakfast lunch dinner
lunch dinner lunch dinner all over. I need a species
I can't read and its entire survival kit: a sky,
a plume puckering red nectar lips.
Need a beak that fits.
Need what I haven't invented. Please,
I need leaving alone, I need pure food
in a thin enough mixture. I need something almost
transparent, right here, that you see
and I don't, you calling *Come quick*
while I'm in the bathroom endlessly
spitting and brushing.

## COUPLE EATING ORANGES
## AFTER DINNER

In his mouth, grinding blind animals
    smash each teardroppy sac,
his tongue, that gummy muscle,
    sorting piths and casings, the inner
skins of the empties collapsed on each other,
    the walls of his throat glopping together
like the word *pulp*, and she's hearing in X-ray, *pulp*,
    in 3-D, *pulp, pulp,* hearing
with her full biome the podge
    on his upper palate, that skullbone
with skin pasted on it,
    hearing a burst, and juice
dribbling down in the dark of his body,
    his prehensile lips already locked
around the next segment-tip,
    his chomp like the joke about how God
must be a civil engineer since who else
    would run a sewer line through a playground,
his orange vanished,
                   hers peeled but still whole,
her globe of juice raw to the air, now she's scraping
    the pith of the peel with her teeth, she's eating it,
she's really eating it, her gulps and muscles
    possibly slo-mo and magnified to him,
though he's clicking around in his puzzle,
    faster, now he's got its trick, and you'd think,
with her embryo ears, her microscope ears,
    she'd hear her own tongue,
but she's in his mudpond and tubes,
    the juice and pulp now slid further inside him,
behind his chest, that broadness
    she will soon lay her head on,

and hear the orange glow of his heat,
    the beat orange becomes
in the wraparound night
    that squeezes and spins
its contents on toward an opening.

## I CAN'T PUT ENOUGH HOUSEHOLD OBJECTS IN THIS POEM TO EQUAL YOUR WONDERFULNESS

You are as perfect an invention as the egg slicer.
You're as pleasing as the first push of the potato masher.
You're the pull through matter, taut wire

and its pane of gold glass cheese. In the galaxy
of countertop crumbs, you're the Goldilocks zone.
You move through rooms. As pleated and rolled

as magazines in the basket, as margin-marked,
fluttered with post-its, as the 600-page book
about weather and art. The drying pajamas,

bottoms and tops, lightly conduct their breezy orchestra
on the one sunny day of late March.
The tiny violets brought in for the windowsill—

though a nose close-up can't smell them,
they ripple the house. One drop in water,
the deep, the paler color. The mouthfeel

of names, barbaresco, manzanilla, tempranillo,
and the labels with animal pictures they say
sell wine best, and we proved them right,

the bright roosters, the charcoaled rabbits and owls.
The buy-six-and-save I bought five of—
how it calls out, how it longs for its ghost,

the corrugated empty slot. And since a pencil
should wait at the end of each reach of my hand,
you're the sharp, the nubbed, the chiaroscuro rub.

Fine as italics, as free as the two-month trial
of the *Times*, so digital, you're brimming, best brew
of coffee, bloom of first foam. Quick mix

of dry and wet, you're the moment
soda and buttermilk meet. You're morning
blazing the windows, long summer evening,

winter's ice, warm as the hat I pull down
on my eyes and ears at night. Are you the cabin
we stayed in by the sea? The mystery I read all stormy day?

You're so wonderful you didn't even speak to me
till it got dark and I closed the book. Question is,
did I then, or ever, as you deserve, look up?

## STARTING AHEAD OF TIME

I set out the breadbowl the night before bread
Days before travel, the suitcase comes down from
    the shelf

I was there early, the empty room, the chairs
with their shining seats in the afternoon sun

I left the house early so not to be rushed
I rushed to be early so as not to rush

Rush the soughing of wind
Rush the rilling of water

The chairs were empty again
staying after

Early while it is quiet
Late while it is quiet

Rushes for candles and rushes
for freshness of floors

My friend who has a different policy
comes late when it's already started

arrives in the middle the people all talking
and leaves while it's still going on

## EQUATION

Subtract the carbon cost of cremation plus shipping
from what will now be unspent of his commute
morning and evening across a long lacy bridge in the fog,

and there's the carbon savings of his death, which
    someone else's
new commute will cancel. And though we see him
    eating soup,
red lentil, with lemon and cumin on top,

someone's got him in a box in the back,
is yelling as she drives, Damn you
for dying, so let's add her mileage

of picking him up at the post office,
diesel to U-Haul his house,
and though we see him biking

a trail between fennel and blackberry walls,
water's whipped glimpses, and quick, at the cross-streets,
the lake's wide sky blue—

he's not in the lab, not
on the bridge, not on the bike, not
in the next chair, but a perfect image of him

is in my brain, his green sweater, his notebook
rubbing a white square in his denim back pocket,
his bass run from E up to G perfectly

present in my ear, his shoulders hunkered
to the beat, and I'm kicking him
for connection, my campaign,

for us to look at each other instead
of our strings or behind our own eyes
when playing the music he's now in the stream of—

except that's my own pulse I'm hearing, my own blood alive,
and the dirt warming up this first spring of him absent,
as many springs past were without us,

though we were not absent then, having not yet
been present, and then, as now, little shouts
perked from the earth, electric and chemical

transmitters chirping and cheeping. There was a radio,
people spoke to each other, ate together,
pulled knee to knee after dinner, crammed into each measure

ornaments and accidentals unhearable
at speed but without which a tune's all surface,
no sub- or unconscious inside it, no cave or star.

And someone gets up for the bathroom,
someone leans out for a smoke,
someone just got here, and our tune,

which you might have thought waved on
past the planets, dings so many molecules
it joins random jostle before even clearing the back fence,

our chairs blipping their white seats
like tabs on a chart, the map we would make
if you attached a flame to us and filmed us in the dark.

## THE PERSON IN THE BOX IS THE ONE

who'd be most thrilled to look, amazed
at the grains, the puzzle
of powder that sticks
to his fingers as they sift: *This,
was this my face?*

Of the absent matter—the sundry, the water—
he'd measure if and where it hovers.
Or, if it hit the stream,
he'd count it jetting, x miles an hour.

If he'd known he was going, he'd have swallowed a trace,
he'd be graphing its path for the conference poster.

He'd be selecting a speck with his favorite tool,
the re-used, autoclaved toothpick,
ends softened and splayed,
be sliding himself under the lens
to make us all look.
*Yeah, yeah,* we'd be, *OK, yeah, cool*—

He'd be shaking the box for the beat, joking around—
*Can you play guitar with my mineral pick?*
He'd add agar agar,
see what would culture.

He'd set it on the nature table in the living room.
So we leave him
at his microscope,
except he's his own microscope,
and of all the jokes anyone's told so far, no one yet
has gotten the one
about the friend and the handful of sand.

## O PIE OF GRACE

Let our flour and butter barely hold,
our liquid be minimal, trust be our motto
for this many icewater tablespoons
no matter how dry, how distracted
our small-pea particles.
Let us be worked fast, our flakiness ever
unthreatened by hand-heat,
and let us in seconds be pressed into rounds,
chill an hour to roll out smooth, our gluten never alerted.
Let us remain tender. Our juices reduce
to fervent fruit flavor, our filling bubble
like baby's first mewling, and let us emerge, golden sun,
our edges artful flutings, our vents like appleseeds,
like violin f-holes, our extra dough
our own decoration, cut cookies of cherries and leaves.
Let us sparkle with sugar.
Let us slice clean,
and be passed to the guests,
our unspilled filling
trembling, gleaming.

Let us be pressed and pressed and never hold.
Let us have been thrown by one in a hurry
in the mechanical bowl, dumped on the blade,
let someone add more, many driblets of any old water.
Let hot palms squash so we can't possibly peel
off sheets of wax paper. Or let our stiff circles
retract and need rolling harder.
Let us burble our pre-verbal goo on the hot oven floor
to burn absolutely, forever black char.
Let the house smell our smoke.
Let our airholes leer, knife-twisted any which way,
our extra trimmings be smashed with a fist, sugared
and blasted like sunburn to crispy snacks. Let our suns

spot and flare, let the spatula bulldoze
our wretched ragged slices, our filling bloop out
on the plate beside a piece too wrecked
to offer a guest, offered anyway,
since what else is there?

## EVERYWHERE IN THE HOUSE

A plastic bag slimy with cilantro
is in the kitchen trash, itself a plastic bag
that would be trash if not stretched upright
by a turquoise can. Shame
for not scraping the black stink
with a silicone scraper into the compost.
Shame for illusion, that silicone's better.
Shame even for the saved and washed—
for having so many saved and washed
waving to dry on chopsticks in a flower frog.

In the mirror, hair of volumizing polymer.
In the practice hour, naturals and accidentals
scaling their plastic steps, half and whole.
In the living room chair, the man with the plastic stent.
In the dish, commemorative flatpicks
stamped with weddings and births.
Delrin, Tortex, we're going for crisp.

It is a container with a snap-on lid.
It is obscure as a bathroom window.
It has moleculed in the rinse cycle.
A bathtub, a duck, a bouncing ball. It is all singing along.
A layer in an impact crater. Return me
to the Great Meteor, plastic my welcome mat,
plastic my digit. Walk with me,
arches of my arches.

It is microfiber calling the dust.
It is laminated to last, a bookmark
lost behind the couch.

Do not tumble in a gust, do not swallow, do not crawl
inside and breathe. When freezing food,

do not top up the plastic box.
Do not jumble, do not wistful, do not
maxopromorphize or minuscule, do not
overlap the stove or wash
the plastic bag by scrubbing with another plastic bag.
It is all freezer-burn and Ziplock.
It did what it could, not enough
to save the cake, now squashed.

## HOW WE SAY GOOD NIGHT
## AFTER A LONG DAY OF WORK

How he looked something up on my laptop
    then washed his hands.
How if he gets sick, he can't visit
    his grandson next week.
How I'm probably no longer contagious
    but my house is a viral zoo. How soap
is a vector. How I will work
    twenty more minutes, then bed. How before bed,
the required routines. How the pages
    the PT printed say 2x a day. How holding the stretch
one minute, reviewing this morning, Maureen in the Ladies',
    wiping her phone with a paper towel, the wad
shedding wet woody threads, how she said
    our phones are the worst
for fecal contamination. How I replied
    that just yesterday, pressing the flusher—
Christ, I've never antibacterialed it. How I shopped
    for a cleaner with no chemical smell,
bought something "biologique," how it reeked
    of rosemary, how here we are waving herbs
at plagues again, washing rings around, and how
    after the twentieth rep, I geranium-soaped,
moldy-sponged, hot-water rinsed the dishes,
    wore lilac rubber gloves. How tired I was,
how it's task after task, how hard
    the viruses labor, how my cough's a gob of living and dead,
how I've coughed and swallowed, blown and wiped
    the stringy yellow, clotted green, clear and thin
of my life my whole life. How ordinary
    to me my own, a stir of stopped and going on.
How I'm servant to the cells, how I filter their wastes.
    How after I'm well I will launder

the sheets I fevered in, how what lived
    in the hot-water tank will sleep with me.

## LYING AWAKE NEXT TO A NOISY SLEEPER

The bed as a field of fumaroles,
viscosity heaving and plopping, fissures
hissing sulphur dioxide.
Tide after tide of vowels
like skinless animals.
Molars grinding like dinosaurs
rolling in gravel. Song of a tomato
pocking pulpy lips, and me
listening so long that metaphor
no longer postpones tuning in
to his literal physical breath.

His vaporous dream words,
his sleep mouth and sleep teeth and sleep tongue
with no clean consonant markers
among the ripples and whispery whistles
that are the actual underground
roaring dark river of language.

The pores in their lacy respiration,
as if this were a nature show, slo-mo, close up,
and we know the scene's coming soon
where predator pounces, and the next scene
will give broader context, habitat,
even the predators threatened. Such suspense
is the reason I never watched *Lassie*, boy and dog
ever in danger, but that wasn't nature, that was a plot
someone wrote, and we're in actual nature—
stars for sure above the roof.
Before bed, believe it, we'd seen the moon

out the backdoor in the thin slice
between neighbor houses.

Where, as here, cells turn over, ticking out, flicking on.
How many cells here in his back and shoulders,
freckles and moles, now breath's ball slams him
hard in the chest—I'm holding mine
till he throws it back—
                              and I return to my theory
that one whose words lose consonants at night
is lucky, for he sleeps.
For consonants are constant wake-up tacks
I count until morning's precisely
four-minute cup.

And now, over hot consonants and toast,
Nature Show, episode two,
actual sun bursting each dot on the window
into elementals of grease and dander,
I'm told I slept, the evidence being my snoring—
a soft snuffling snore, a very sweet snore,
a snore nonetheless.
So in all the night's splatted batter,
the other, awake, had been listening.
Such a pair of pancakes,
bubbles on top, bottom burning.

## WHAT I HAVE INSTEAD

Instead of love, I have a tangent. I have to write it
right now on a Post-it. I haven't remembered
our special love moments, but I have that redwood
color of wine. I have jokes we both know,
have practiced and confirmed: anything's funnier
with the word *silage* inserted.

Of your childhood, I have vignettes, the broken
magic trick, the father fallen at the rink. I have to look
out the window right now, the tree
with its hushing dark branches.
Instead of love, I have its environs: green paintings
and wool braided rug, very cozy.
I have to jump up to make an adjustment.

And for our breakfast, I have good butter,
our favorite slightly sour bread. In the snow,
I had an unshoveled driveway, had shirked civic duty
for liability. I have heard
from across a valley
the sound of a stone down a mountain.
Have listened for it daily.
I have to rise early.

Not love, but lists. Ingredients
for the Meyer lemon pizza anniversary.
Wait, I have to turn off the timer.
I have to lower the heat to simmer.

Instead of a heart, I have good hearing,
chitters everywhere, and silver pain
in every elevator ding.
I have what I don't tell you, which is

nothing special but all so internal.
You hear me in the bathroom pour the saltwash through.

I have your same tangle of grays and each week
more white. I have some years of a tree,
the maple's sticky new leaves
creaking open each spring. Instead of saying
those words you say to me,
I say before dinner, *Read to me while I chop.*
I say after dinner, *Hand me the pencil sharpener, please.*
I say in bed when you begin reading aloud
the book that makes us laugh—Joke, I don't speak—
I'm already asleep—and what I say next
in the morning is *Don't talk, I'm trying to remember my dream.*

If I had a heart, and if it had cockles,
they'd be warmed by our crossouts and circles,
drafts for the cartoon caption contest.
How we racked ourselves for it,
what one mouse says to the other
as they ponder the instructions for assembly
on the box of the maze kit.

## WOMAN GOING GRAY

Her smashed clay vases of hair,
her briquets of hair at the hottest ash,
her hurry, slap-the-meat-on hair.
Her jingling ring of master keys hair.

Her Theosophist hair knocking from under the table,
her tea-leaf, parentheses, commas of hair,
all the thirty-second notes in her hair, triplets and jigs
    of hair,

her hair's early violets, her hair's hanging clusters
of heavy sweet grapes.

Her hair of thimbles, her pearl button hair,
her long-eyed and round-eyed needles of hair.

Her hair of begonias looming from fog.

Her hair of sap gleaming between plates of pinebark hair,
bristlecone, hardscrabble,
hair of the bird-names, flower-names, stones.

Her every fabric and skill of hair, archery, herringbone,
go, get a move-on hair.

All the shrugs in her hair.
All the sleeping fish in her hair.
Driftwood, searocket, oar and plash
of her hair, her hair
still looking out the window in the morning.

Her hair of white avalanche lilies.
Hair of the flashlight eyes, deer
and unconfirmed sightings

of maybe-extinct panther hair,
voles in their burrow, her hair
in the pellets of barred owls, her blizzard
hair blundered halfway to the barn.

## HOW LONG HAVE YOU BEEN TEACHING BANJO?

I've traded lessons for my kitchen mixer gears
to be packed with new grease.
Since then, decades of birthday cakes.
Traded lessons for porch steps made wrong,
the all-wood support after one year
melting to grass. Trading time
for music but which of us gets which?

*Can I have a shorter lesson for less?*
*Can I have a longer lesson for more?*
Every lesson is long and won't ever be over.

I played them the sources.
Took them as far as the past was recorded.
Their names in notebooks,
and under each name, tune titles and dates.

*The sound isn't written*, I said. I said, *Listen,*
*which note is higher?* I said, *Trace the string*
*with your finger up to the peg.*
I said, *Think of strings at the peghead*
*opening into a flower.*

*Swing your arm*, I say, *like walking down the road.*
*Road*, I say, never *sidewalk* or *street*.
*One-and, two-and* I taught time,
*and-one*, move *and* to the start.
*Play the pattern while gazing at nature or art.*
*No flicking your finger. Try holding small fruit,*
*a lime or a winter Satsuma. Or library card or museum card.*
I will never say *credit card*.
*Find the melody. Be methodical,*

*each string open, each string fret by fret.*
Why, every time, do they skip the one note they want?

Of the worried one who froze at each mistake,
I asked, *What will happen when you get it right?*

A friend's T-shirt says *What part of bum-diddy don't you
 understand?*
but I ask *Do you have a pet?*
I say, *cute puppy, big kitty* and once,
*green parrot, green parrot,* silky emerald
on the student's shoulder.

I have taught a bone doctor who traded me a window.
I have taught a radiologist who retired yesterday but still
knows cancer when she sees it.
I have taught an oceanographer at his melanoma end
hourly drinking last-ditch raw juice,
who gave me a cookbook he wrote
with his wife, a Russian prosodist of English verse—
how spattered now, the page of my life's best borscht?

The highschooler hands me the fee
his parents have tucked in his case,
plus a ten-dollar tip.
*No need to give extra*, I said, and he said,
*My parents told me to tell you,
music teachers are holy.*

What could I do? I took the money.

The notebooks with their names
go in what kind of museum?
Handwritten artifacts, hand-collaged covers.
Now a digital file for each one.

I've taught a man and twenty years later his son.
A mother traded her three children
to their father for one hour of banjo class.
I've taught a leader of love studies
who absolutely would not listen.
I agreed on a trade with a tree-man
who pruned my hundred-foot fir, and still owe him hours
for his sawing and haulage, but he never called back,
the branches shaggier now than before him.

## CLEMATIS MISS BATEMAN

This flower squinch its prickly whiskernose, winching itself, this flower wide its surprise, freckle its aim, this flower's mauve grabbers going *Yikes yikes*, this flower battening backward as if wind, this flower paddling the air, this flower speaking *Gong gong gong I'm talking to you, yes, you*, this flower tuning higher, higher, this flower fed up.

This flower a pang, this flower with eyelashes painted outside its eyelashes and eyelashes painted outside its painted eyelashes, this flower white on what, hinting darker or purple, what color exactly, evening's inner shell, a washed and washed ancient bandage, an estate sale's curdled lavender lotion.

This flower an emergency, this flower still pinching and pursing, this flower going *Hey hey HEY*, it's turning into a Cezanne, it's slapping flat palms on the flat pan of sky, it's ignoring its crippled one and crispy browns, this flower floating its eyeballs into space, this flower filamental.

This flower will do anything *anything*, rattling its shaker, this flower blasting from Cape Canaveral, this flower sitting here like a plate on the table just waiting, this flower catching the microdrifts, this flower's fat face staring up at, *What, you wanna make something of it?* who cares a blink, this hummy flower at your cheek, this homing bomb.

## WHAT HAVE YOU NOT DONE YET?

Not yet floated in the Gold Band lily's creamy songs,
nor glistened in Apricot Queen's core chartreuse.

The silk-wrapped bee-shell hangs mid-pollen in the Lucifer,
and I have not been a spider, have not addressed the
    shivering center.

When summer solstice went all fuschia on lavender-copper,
    did I linger?
Leaping for the next minute, that long rippling evening,

I roofed myself under. And I will have died still owing letters
to a stage-four friend predicted passed by now, but every spring,

found lambing in the barn. As long as lambs are borning,
she can't die. You and I did not do our intimacy exercise,

did not even dip in step one. At every memorial, praise—
What a heart, what a friend. And in the car home, we agree

what matters: They held you in their clear attention.
Your turn, my turn, ten minutes each, honestly,

the lilies don't care if I love, that's why I sit spiced
in their perfume. Though something's amiss in their soil—

What purples the stalks? what leathers the leaves?
For the third summer, I have not IDed the key mineral.

Nor have I crazed the dishes at the shard required
for none of each set, beyond me, to trouble

my brother's cupboard. Have not bottomsed-up
the blue curaçao my mother left. Save the last drop

for my closing salve. And still have not said words of love.
Let us make art under the drift of the lilies,

their brick-dark powder shading my shoulders,
the gold of their hurtle to spill more lilies

harping my hair. Seeing me there, no one could know,
but truly, I wept for dearness of friends. But for you,

in this, my only flame, I can't rise softly orange enough,
can't set orchid violet enough—*There'll be another chance /*

*this be the last.* I have sung that refrain
but not grieved in its gloaming.

I have not chanted *pistil* and *style*
till they fractal into multi-colored glass.

## WHAT TO DO WITH A BOX OF FOLDERS,

each tab a noun in her handwriting,
    Bristlecone pine,
        Coulter Pine,
her sketches,
    Rabbit,
        Saxifrage,
the box in the closet since she died,
two cubic feet we need for our stuff,
but these unfinished, what to do, her pencil
having been on the page,
her hand on the pencil,
eye on the flower,
    the seal and seal pups in the ocean,
        the pines in the mountains,
her feet on the trail,
the tabs on the folders,
each folder with one or five or a few
sketches or not even a sketch, a line
smooth or rugged, the words on the tabs
the order of thought,
alphabetical,
    Cattle,
        Cormorants,
            Dogs,
categorical,
    Yellow Pine,
        Monterey Cypress,
           White Oak,
impossible,
    Aspen 1961,
        Glen Canyon 1960,
to order by year or location or letter,
some simple ink gestures,
some watercolor washes,

some cross-section diagrams,
do we really need that box-shape
of space for ourselves,
for what, for something important
like a broken lamp or important
as molecules move—
so we might move them—
write letters on the backs or fold
them into library books,
and before they leave us, enveloped, addressed,
or chanced to those who check out our same books,
we'll scan them and set our preferences
for the screensaver,
keeping just a few on paper—
    nettle,
        otter,
            monkeyflower—
to glue each year
on the cover of the calendar,
to glue each year
at the index of the bullet book.

## IN MY DREAM IT'S ALWAYS A WOODEN HOUSE

setting and map and container
the house a wood layout
divided like silverware drawers

bedrooms and bedrooms off bedrooms
hallways off hallways a room
to pass through to the bath
stairs to a narrower landing
and landings to cross to a door

round windows like finches
round windows like brown shoes

a cabin not far from the river
a cul-de-sac raw new construction
a house under trees in a clearing

balcony air and a cubby-hole under the stairs
each room an egg in tissue in its box

the dust of wood the slow billow of wood
the shrill sap yellow feather of wood
wood tread and wood riser
the wood pocket doors
the old and new smell of the wood
the pocket breadboards quiet in their slots

the windows with unfinished sashes
the front door half-planed and sandpaper waiting
the hinges' brass leaves lying open

the wood door off its pins
a person inside at their work can be seen
in a frame by anyone passing but no one passes

the woodsap walls and the window open to woods
the morning wood table
the house breathing steam from the roof

## THERE WILL BE BEAUTY

But it won't be these green slants of water, grass in the
    river canyon, won't
be the waterbirds swooping the grass. Already isn't the
    brimming,

already isn't solid with homeward fish. Even now, and despite,
it is sometimes a dam, even now, sunset and glory of arches.

There will be beauty, but not these birds, their own senses
inside them, cool swallows of air, how it tastes to them,

summer's thick brack. Beauty, and it might remain
these shapes of brown hill, and the shadows, like rags,

of clouds ranging the slopes. Absent the birds, it won't
    be the sips
in the birds, or how, on the twigs of their legs,

it feels, a breaking line of water. Nor their ride down the air
to this valley's flats and draws, their skid and white wake,

their rise, settle, rise, no rest, no rest
of return. There will be beauty of movement, already is,

of billow, cling, float,
beauty of speck, of longing, already,

beauty of rocks. Of a washed
and washed stick. Of suspense, of the sun

expanding, of soon, a white dwarf. Beauty of remnant, of
    cooling.
We want to say something of our lives under these scrolling
    clouds, over

the yellows, in the brown ditches—Did we live, were we ever
inside ourselves, sipping? Were we beauty, drawing spark
    from splinter,

orange from iron, each of us thatching the roofs of our
    burning decisions?
Never knew how, still learning how, but we loved beauty,
    tried to become it,

were grateful to all of it, and if it was going, if it was already—
*Did we miss it? No, I just saw it. Did you dream it? Swear, I*
    *saw it—*

we still time our time by it, still looking up to it, wishing
the heat would hurry through beauty of thirst, beauty

where birds with no field must keep flying. Beauty of gases,
wish we could see it, the sun's red enfolding, could have the eyes

of ourselves without ourselves, earth encompassed, beauty
of eon, of mineral, creatures millennia gone.

## THEY FIND ME

On the grass beneath the feeder, among the sunflower hulls.
In my sock feet, hand on half a catnip mouse.

They've found my calendula, teaspoon.
They've found my cuspid and dipthong.
Out the window, traces on the bushes
where pomace was tossed after crushing.

Where the thieves bring the gold,
by tooth, by cufflink,
dropping it, plop by plop,
in the cauldron for melting—

after the pouring off, they find me
at the bottom of the pot.

All this time, I've been searching the world
for the stolen rings that were my mother's.

They knew me by the shoe caught in the chain of the swing.
On my face, an expression of curly brackets.

What are the odds the leaf would fall directly on the lyre?
What are the odds that through the missing
bottom of a teacup in the sea, a bright red fish would swim?

A string plucked in the room behind them made them turn.
When they found me, I was in a boat,
they could not believe it, I was still rowing.

## NOTES

"April 4–June 18" and "There was no one moment": In memoriam, Jean E. Tenenbaum, 1928 - 2008.

"Banjo, Banjo on the Wall":

> For all banjo makers and players, unknown and known, past and present.
>
> Stanza 1: "Why do you fly so high, wings so blue": The song, "Little Birdie," has been played by many and with a variety of verses, but I'm thinking of The Coon Creek Girls:
>
>> Little birdie, little birdie, why do you fly so high?
>>
>> It's because I have a true little heart, and I don't care to die.
>
> My first banjo was a rented plastic Kay.
>
> Stanza 2: A sock or rag can be stuffed in the back of a banjo to dampen the overtones. What poet could resist the names of banjo players, for instance, Matokie Slaughter, of Pulaski, Virginia. "Can I play your sugarpast banjo?": Enslaved Africans and their descendants developed the banjo on sugar plantations in the Caribbean. See *The Banjo: America's African Instrument,* by Laurent DuBois, and *Well of Souls: Uncovering the Banjo's Hidden History,* by Kristina R. Gaddy. What is a Los Angeles-born Jewish girl doing playing this instrument?
>
> Stanza 4: Cat's Ass banjo by Jere Canote. Plieades/lighthouse banjo and wildflower banjo by Paul Hostetter (1945–2019). In memoriam for him, and with much sorrow also for the fire-damaged forests around Santa Cruz, California.

Stanza 5: "dents my breasts./…tore my shorts." A banjo can be brutal. "Padded, stonewashed": Banjo pad for protecting the player's lap, designed and sewn by Martha Thompson.

Stanza 6: More banjo players: Etta Baker, Kyle Creed, Blanche Coldiron.

Stanza 8: Ekonting—West African gourd-bodied stringed instrument. Possibly the ekonting (also called *akonting*) is one of the instruments the enslaved held in memory as they worked with available materials to create instruments that would become known as banjos.

Stanza 9: Most tunes in this genre have 32 bars, though there are many exceptions. The banjo's 5th string is shorter than the others and is droned with the thumb. Plangent, incessant, harmonizing with and gritting against an ongoing melody.

"My Father Would Have Loved the Internet": In memoriam, Morton Tenenbaum, 1923–1984. "Series of too-small boxes": See "Many too small boxes and Maru" on You Tube.

"My brother's face": On September 24, 2015, a Ride the Ducks vehicle on the Aurora Bridge in Seattle veered across the center line and crashed into a bus carrying North Seattle College International Students who had just arrived from their countries and were touring the city a few days before the start of Fall quarter. Five were killed and many injured. Honoring those who died in the crash: Claudia Derschmidt, 49 of Austria (visiting her student son); Privando Putradanto, 18, of Indonesia; Runjie Song, 17, of China; Mami Sato, 36, of Japan; and

Kim Ha Ram, 20, of South Korea. And with deepest love for Dan Tenenbaum, his boundless heart.

"Do We Gripe?": For Martha Silano. With memories of Bar 717 Ranch.

"To an Aunt in Another City"; "Works on Paper"; "Heard from Inside the Ashes Box";"Before Storing Her Paintings under My Bed"; "Well, she died with them under her own bed"; "What to do with a box of folders": In memoriam, Frances Thompson, beloved Auntie Fran, 1933 – 2014.

"Pass the Salt": for Ruthie Dornfeld, Margo Murphy, and Hilary Scull Hart.

"What I Have Instead": The caption we came up with was "Oh no! It says *Cheese not included*!"

"Equation": In memoriam, Dan Lockshon 1955-2013. And for Margo Murphy, Laura Lockshon, and all the Queen City Bulldogs (me, Armin Barnett, David Cahn, Dan Lockshon). In the background may be heard "Will the Circle Be Unbroken" as sung by the Monroe Brothers: "One by one, their seats were emptied, / One by one, they went away. / Now our circle has been broken / Will it be complete one day?"

"The Person in the Box": Dan Lockshon.

"How Long Have You Been Teaching Banjo?": With gratitude to all my music students over the years: Thank you for the chance to pass something along. And for Maggie Lind, who invented *big kitty*.

"What Have You Not Done Yet?": In stanza 2, Crocosmia 'Lucifer.'

"There Will Be Beauty": Road trip home to Seattle from Weiser, Idaho, across eastern Oregon and eastern Washington. For Dan Tenenbaum and for Stickerville.

## ACKNOWLEDGMENTS

Many thanks to the journals where these poems, sometimes in other versions, first appeared.

*Alaska Quarterly Review*: "My brother's face";

*BP Review*: "Everywhere in the House";

*Cimmarron Review*: "Nine-Year-Old Girl Meets Picasso's Weeping Woman with a Handkerchief";

*The Cortland Review*: "Sounds Heard from Inside the Ashes Box";

*Crab Creek Review*: "After She Died, I Saw the Skull in Everyone," "Woman Going Gray";

*Disquieting Muses Quarterly*: "But a Cat Is Always in the Room," "There Will Be Beauty";

*Ecotone*: "I'm Tired of Life and Death," "How Long Have You Been Teaching Banjo?";

*Moria*: "I Can't Put Enough Household Objects in This Poem to Equal Your Wonderfulness";

*North American Review*: "Pass the Salt";

*Poetry Northwest*: "The Arborists," "My Father Would Have Loved the Internet," "We Used to Lose Our Nozzles All the Time," "Works on Paper";

*The Shore*: "They Find Me," "What to do with a box of folders," "What Have You Not Done Yet?";

*Small Orange*: "The White Wing";

*Southern Humanities Review*: "I Need a Hummingbird";

*Water~Stone Review*: "O Pie of Grace."

Bright waving banners and flapping buntings of gratitude to Sharon Bryan: Without her wisdom, without the openness and curiosity of her reading and conversation, this book could not have found its shape.

Martha Silano, friend and companion-in-poems: Thank you for all the conversations—the here-and-there, the this-and-that of connection and disjunction among the many things.

Deep bows to honor the late David Wagoner, my first teacher in my first workshop on my first day of the University of Washington MFA program, who gave me the benefit of the doubt.

## ABOUT THE AUTHOR

Molly Tenenbaum is the author of four previous books of poems: *Mytheria* (Two Sylvias, 2017); *The Cupboard Artist* (Floating Bridge, 2012); *Now* (Bear Star, 2007); and *By a Thread* (Van West & Co., 2000). Her chapbook/artist book, *Exercises to Free the Tongue* (2014), a collaboration with artist Ellen Ziegler, combines poems with archival materials about her grandparents, ventriloquists on the vaudeville circuit. Her poems have appeared in *The Alaska Quarterly Review, The Beloit Poetry Journal, Best American Poetry, New England Review, the North American Review, Poetry, Poetry Northwest, Prairie Schooner*, and elsewhere.

She grew up in Los Angeles, influenced by the Pacific Ocean, English-major parents, Westland School, the Mulholland chapparal, and the Los Angeles County Museum of Art; by folk music events of the region: The UCLA Folk Festival, The San Diego Folk Festival, The Topanga Canyon Banjo and Fiddle Contest; and by the concerts, lessons, and community at McCabe's Guitar Shop. Moving northward, she earned a BA from the

Hutchins School of Liberal Studies at Sonoma State University and an MFA at the University of Washington.

Her recordings of old-time Appalachian banjo are *The Hillsides Are All Covered with Cakes*, *Instead of a Pony* and *Goose & Gander*. She lives in Seattle, having taught English at North Seattle College for 30+ years, currently teaching music in the living room and at Dusty Strings Music School. Find her at mollytenenbaum.com and at mollytenenbaum.bandcamp.com.

CPSIA information can be obtained
at www.ICGtesting.com
Printed in the USA
LVHW111226230223
740172LV00005B/227